Hearts & Hands

One Woman's Journey To Create
a Better Future For Children

Adedolapo Osuntuyi

Copyright © 2024

The rights of Adedolapo Osuntuyi to be identified as the author of this work has been asserted by her in accordance with the copyright laws.

All rights reserved.

No part of this publication may be reproduced, stored in a retrieval system or transmitted in any form or by any means, electronic, mechanical, photocopying, recording or otherwise without the prior permission of the author or publisher.

Cover Design: BramoDigi

Layout Design and Prints by:
Heart2World Publishing
Ago Palace Way. Lagos
w. heart2worldpublishing.org
t. 09056183960
e. heart2worldpublishing@gmail.com

For information on distribution, translation or bulk sales, please contact:

Adedolapo Osuntuyi
Phone: +234-708-739-0017, +234-912-475-3760
Email: adedolapo@dollychildrenfoundation.org

Book Reviews

The depth of gratitude that I owe the author is boundless because right from her childhood she has shown to be a special and spiritual child of God in all her undertakings.

I've been filled with immense joy seeing the projects of Dolly Children Foundation moving from being just an idea to becoming a reality.

It is interesting to read this book as the benefits of good education should be targeted at the most impoverished in the society. More crucially, this book helps one to get a greater understanding of what a good foundation for NGOs and anyone concerned about creating change in the society should be.

I am convinced that anyone across the world that will pick up Dolapo Osuntuyi's book will find answers to pressing questions in their hearts. None is likely to put it down disappointed.

Prince S. A. Oladimeji

"Hearts and Hands" details an incredible journey into Dolapo's world of selfless service to under-served children in the poorest communities.

Dolapo's well crafted and moving style transports you alongside her into communities where she has touched and positively changed lives forever.

She takes us on her adventures, her seemingly insurmountable struggles and strivings, but we celebrate her victories too as she toils hard for educational equality for under-served children everywhere she meets them.

One is able to share her deep sense of unease and mortification at the neglect the children suffer, and the inadequacies and detachment of relevant institutions towards making the necessary changes to the plight and sufferings of these young ones.

Hearts and Hands is a deeply inspiring book, we are challenged to do more to help children, to serve children, particularly in poor communities, so they can access good quality education as well as every benefit required to raise wholesome children to become a source of pride to their nation and the world.

This beautiful story of social transformation and positive impact does not leave us clueless as to how to advance the cause of Dolly Children Foundation.

In the latter chapters of the book, Dolapo shares a number of ways we can each or collectively get our hands in and support this worthy and noble cause.

I trust we are moved to do so. To reuse a quote from the book "Not all of us can do great things, but we can all do small things with great love" - Mother Theresa. And in the words of a gospel song, may the Lord lead us in His love to those around us.

Mrs Ireti Olutayo
Board Chair, Dolly Children Foundation

The book left me very inspired. Wow! Your journey is so inspiring and you have come such a long long way.

This book will definitely inspire people to live a fulfilled and selfless life of giving. Thank you so much for documenting your journey to be as detailed as possible.

This book will help people trace their life's journey to find their purpose and pursue GOD's plan and assignment for their lives boldly.

I also like that you included the importance of self care which is something that most people, especially leaders, pay little attention to.

This book is amazing. I had goosebumps while reading.

It really lighted in me a zeal to serve and follow GOD's plan per time.

Aramide Kayode
Founder, Talent Mine Academy

Wow! This book is incredible and the story behind it is definitely one I would recommend to all my friends who are thinking of starting projects or NGOs.

Often times, we only see on Instagram and Facebook how Dolly Children Foundation is making children smile, but we don't see the pain and other successes that happen behind the scene. I love how Dolapo also walked us through from her childhood, her father's story, to her university education down to when she began the foundation.

Starting an NGO may not be rocket science, but to be successful at it, one needs to be like a rocket engine, firing on all cylinders while aiming for quality and the highest impact possible. There will be times when your rocket will feel as though it's running out of fuel but in Dolapo's words: "When your heart is filled with a genuine desire to give, resources have a way of finding their way into your hands."

Mirabelle Morah
Founder, Blankpaperz Media

'Hearts and Hands' is a practical guide for young leaders. Dolapo has leveraged storytelling to arm us with insights for finding our purpose, mobilising support and doing excellent work that makes life better for others. This insightful read takes you along her unique journey and leaves you with actionable steps for life and living.

If you're unsure of your next steps or you're getting burned out in your current life season, this book will rekindle your zeal and encourage you. Thank you Dr. Dolapo *(as I like to call you)* for this amazing resource.

Ugochi Obidiegwu
Founder, The Safety Chic & UGIP Development Foundation

I have known Adedolapo for over a decade and reading *Hearts and Hands* is a true reflection of her tenacity and dogged determination in the face of challenges. Her book speaks to her vision for DCF and showcases her compassion while navigating the steps she undertook to fulfil her purpose. *Hearts and Hands* is an insightful story of how one's experiences can shape and alter one's dreams and aspirations.

I hope you enjoy this book like I did.

Mrs Omowunmi Sanni
Partner, Duale, Ovia & Alex-Adedipe

Not all of us can do great things, but we can do small things with great love.

- Mother Theresa

Dedication

This book is dedicated to everyone who strives to make a positive impact on the world, one child at a time.

Acknowledgement

Writing "Heart and Hands" has been a journey I never imagined undertaking. I owe immense gratitude to those who have played a pivotal role in bringing this book to life.

First, I express my deepest appreciation to my Dad, whose story of hope, resilience, and determination laid the foundation for what is today known as the Dolly Children Foundation. Your unwavering strength and drive has been the fuel for my passion in advocating for equitable education.

To my husband, Ifedayo, I am profoundly thankful for your constant support throughout this endeavour. Your encouragement, understanding, and patience have been my pillars of strength.

I extend my sincere thanks to Oluwatobi Adesanya, my Publisher, and Abraham Ologundudu who designed the book cover. Your invaluable guidance, expertise, and collaboration have enriched the essence of this book and elevated its content.

To wrap up, this book is a culmination of collective efforts, and I am humbled by the support and contributions of each individual. Thank you for being part of this remarkable journey.

To my family and community of friends, thank you for your unwavering support and dedication to nurturing young minds and shaping the future.

To the resilient, curious children who inspire me every day, thank you.

And finally, to every person who dares to dream big and create meaningful change, this book is for you.

Content

Book Reviews	3
Dedication	11
Acknowledgement	12
Author's note	17

Chapter One: 19

     The Genesis

Chapter Two: 33

     Finding My Path

Chapter Three: 53

     Challenges of Education in Nigeria

Chapter Four: 67

     Launching Dolly Children Foundation

Chapter Five: 79

     The Work Life Balance

Chapter Six: 89

    The Art of Intentional Giving

Chapter Seven: 99

    The Hands That Help and Lift

Programs and activities 132

About the author 133

Author's Note

As a child, the idea of running a foundation for kids never crossed my mind. I was fortunate to have a great support system which included my parents, a couple of family members, and a number of close knitted friends. My life's story unfolded in a way that led me down the path I'm now on - the path of making a significant impact in the lives of children.

I was set on this path by my parents and the schools I attended. I also came to realise that every experience I had growing up, shaped every bit of the story you're about to read.

At the core of my journey is my love for education and its capacity to bring meaningful and measurable transformation to the lives of children anywhere in the world.

Now, after working with children for nearly two decades, it's crystal clear that education isn't just getting a certificate, it is refining the soul, the mindset, and the overall outlook a person has on life. Society is made better when people are educated.

I believe so much in the power of education to transform a child who the world has looked down on into a person, a community, a nation, and, by extension, the entire world. In the words of Nelson Mandela, "Education is the most powerful weapon that you can use to change the world." I believe this too.

My father's story, as you would read in the opening chapter of this book, was like a seed sown skillfully by a farmer that would eventually bud into what has become the story of the Dolly Children Foundation.

With this, I invite you on a journey to the beautifully evolving story of my life and my life's dream, the Dolly Children Foundation.

Adedolapo Osuntuyi

Chapter **One**

The Genesis

"The best thing about existence is that any moment in time can be a point of beginning to anything!"

- Mehmet Murat Ildan

CHAPTER ONE

Like every child with big dreams, in my growing years, I desired to study medicine at the university. It had been my dream all along to see myself in white overalls, a stethoscope dangling across my neck, and operating on bodies in the theatre. I just loved the idea of saving lives and giving people a better chance to live healthy, whole, and happy. What better way could I achieve this dream than to become a medical doctor? It was a no-brainer, at least I thought. But life had other plans for me. Despite my aspirations, when the time came to take the compulsory JAMB (Joint Admission Matriculation Board) exams that year, my scores fell short of the required cut-off mark for medicine. My hopes were dashed!

My aunt and her husband, who I fondly refer to as Mummy & Daddy Fatade, desired that I make the most of the time I had on my hands, so they purchased a pre-degree form for me at Lagos State University. I went for the pre-degree program and much later I was offered admission to study Botany.

As I stood at the notice board, looking at my name on the admission list, I couldn't help but feel disappointed. Botany? How could I study Botany when my initial desire was to become a medical doctor? All my life, I had dreamed of becoming a doctor, helping people, and making a real difference in the world. And now, because I had failed to reach the cut-off mark, I now had to study plants instead? The upside to this curve ball that life had thrown at me was that studying botany would be a 4-year programme as opposed to studying for 7 years to qualify as a medical doctor, but this was not to be.

The classes began and while I was trying to wrap my hands around my love for plants, this 4-year programme quickly stretched to a 7-year programme. It so happened that when I was in my 200L, I had already spent 5 years. Why? Because of the constant industrial strike action across the country. Either the university staff were protesting an increase in salaries, or the university commission was nationally getting into loggerheads with the government over some policy or even student crises and unrest on campus. It was devastating, to say the least.

Despite this setback, I came to realise there is a miraculous way God shows up in dark and gloomy moments to give us light and direction. He gives a sense of purpose and meaning even in the middle of challenges we may feel helpless to solve.

I started to have very descriptive dreams where I saw the late Pastor Bimbo Odukoya, Pastor Sam Adeyemi, Pastor E. A. Adeboye and a host of other notable people having conversations with me. At other times, I saw myself carrying crying children from the hands of their parents and when I carried them, they would immediately stop crying. Children, much like plants, are tender and require love and affection to thrive and become all they were created to be. I can clearly trace the genesis of this story to a number of events from my childhood; every one of these happenings was by no means coincidental. I believe they were orchestrated divinely to bring me into purpose. It started with...

My Classmate's Journal

I had a friend in school who was also my classmate. I knew her right from JSS 1. At the beginning of every term, she and other students were always brought in on three different buses branded with the name of an orphanage. I knew there had to be a story behind it, but I never asked. Just before one of the long holiday breaks (we were in JSS 3 at this time), I discovered something.

She had a journal which she guarded so jealously and wouldn't let anyone even take a look at it. On this very day, she had forgotten something in the hostel, went to pick it up and left her locker open. I seized my chance, reached for her locker, picked up the book and rifled through the pages. This was not something I'd ordinarily do. It wasn't a practice for me to go through people's things, but my curiosity had reached its peak.

Written in her own handwriting were the details of her escape from the brutal Liberian war, how her parents had died in the chaos, and how she had survived by eating different kinds of grass to stay alive as she traversed the country in search of help. Her journey had led her to Nigeria, where she united with her brother and they ended up at the same orphanage. While her brother attended another school, she attended my own school, being an all-girls school.

Though I was about 13 years old, reading her story and now seeing how it was through this orphanage that she had a chance to rebuild her life, shook me to my core. It helped me see the incredible work her orphanage was doing. That day, I came to know that orphanages make a huge difference in the lives of underprivileged children. I saw how orphanages help children who have no access to help or resources become who they have the potential to be. With this story lingering in my mind, I left school that day and returned home for the long holiday break.

Back at home

I had more than enough stories to tell everyone. From how I needed a new pair of sandals to reading my classmate's journal, and a whole lot more.

At the time, my dad worked as an accountant with the Federal Civil Service and was often posted to different states to work. On the day I returned home, he came in tired, but was excited to see his little, beloved daughter. We hugged and exchanged pleasantries, but this night was different. By 9 p.m., my father began narrating the story of his life to me like he had never done before. There was so much intentionality on this very day that I stayed glued to him till he was done.

My Father's Story Inspired Me

On March 31, 1948, my father, Prince Simeon Adebowale Oladimeji, was born in Ekiti, Nigeria (a state in the south west). It was a battle for him from the beginning and one of the battles he had to face was overcoming poverty.

My father's life began in a world that was recovering from the horrors of the Second World War and in a nation that was still under British colonialism. In his words that day, he said, *"I was born into poverty. I saw it clearly. I experienced everything poverty could be called and I do not wish anyone experiences it anymore."* He knew that his only hope for a better life was education. Thankfully, the government established free education in 1955, and at the age of 7, he began school without shoes.

This was the era where students had to be able to touch their left ears with their right hand to qualify as students. No student was admitted into school without passing this simple test. When my dad passed, he was handed a black slate and a chalk and made to sit on the floor with other children. This was his giant step towards a brighter future—a significant moment for him; he now had his ticket out of poverty.

In 1960, Nigeria gained its independence, and that same year, he completed his primary education. Though he was happy about this, he had no means to continue his education. His uncle from Kabba (present day Kogi State) visited during that time and promised to enrol him in a secondary school if he followed him. Joyfully, my father followed, but after two whole years had passed, the promise had not been fulfilled. Determined not to let go of his dreams, my father composed a letter to his uncle which was sent via the post office.

When his uncle received the letter, he assumed his mother dictated the contents of the letter to someone skilled enough to write. The letter was a clever ploy to escape his grip. His plan worked.

Once back in Ekiti, my father gave the 5 pounds he had received from his uncle to his dad to keep so that he wouldn't spend it. His intention was to use the money as part payment for his enrollment fees into secondary school. Unfortunately, the money was spent by his dad, dashing the hopes of enrolling in school. But he didn't quit! Left with no one to help him, my dad decided to learn tailoring for 6 months while seeking out possible ways for him to raise funds to enrol in a secondary school.

Luck shined on him when an uncle came from Port Harcourt, a state in the southern part of Nigeria, to pick him up with the intention of sponsoring him through school. He was put into a school there but not too long after, the Civil War started and everyone was asked to return to their respective towns of origin.

When he returned home, still burning with the desire for education, he visited a friend of his, the late Mr. Michael

Ogunyebi, who was privileged to be in a secondary school. This friend of his borrowed him books for three years on different subjects like commerce, economics, government, bookkeeping, English, Mathematics and politics. These books opened up new worlds for my father, and he devoured them eagerly.

After three years, he had his O-level certification without even stepping into a secondary school. With his certification, he was employed as a proof-reader in Daily Sketch at Ibadan and was posted to Abeokuta as a commercial manager at a Daily Sketch branch office in Abeokuta, where he spent 3 years before he travelled out of the country. This job afforded him the opportunity to meet many important personalities. Through these contacts, he was able to get them to pay for advertisements for their events in the newspaper company he worked for. With his income, he saved up enough money to travel abroad.

After securing his visa, he went on to pursue an accounting and finance degree, graduating from South-Eastern University in 1979. He later pursued a Master's degree in Finance. He was in the United States of America between 1976 and 1982, after which the Federal Civil Service went to the US to recruit him and several other graduates for employment with the Nigerian government. (In those days, the Federal Government usually travelled out to bring the best brains back home to work for the country.) When he moved back to Nigeria, he landed a job with the Federal Government as an accountant in the Ministry of Finance and Economic Development. He was there until he retired as an assistant director.

My father's story taught me that education was—and still is—a powerful tool to break the chains of poverty. Despite facing many challenges and setbacks, he never gave up on his dreams. His determination, resourcefulness, and love for learning enabled him to overcome obstacles and achieve his goals.

On this very day, looking in admiration at my father with tears in his eyes and mine after a three-hour conversation, there was an aura of accomplishment and spark in his eyes. This struck an impression in my heart as a little girl and that evening, a firm desire to promote education as a key to changing lives was birthed in me.

That same night, amidst his tears, he said, "I do not want you to grow up to become a liability to anyone." Then he jolted out of his seat and asked me to kneel, and then, out of his heart, he rained words of prayer on me in a way I'd never seen before. It was years later that I knew, without a doubt, that my destiny was tied to his and that I had a calling to fulfil. I dare say that that experience with my father sparked this movement.

The Newspaper Article

Reading my classmate's journal and being prayed for by my dad, set me on the right path.

As fate would have it, during the holidays, I found myself idly flipping through the pages of a newspaper when a headline caught my eye. The orphanage of this classmate of mine, whose journal I had read weeks before, was celebrating her anniversary. In doing so, they chose to celebrate three of their outstanding children and she was one of them. As I read it, it felt like I was reading the success story of something I would do in the future.

Something stirred deep within me, and I felt a sudden surge of compassion and purpose. I closed my eyes and whispered a prayer: *"God, please give me the strength and means to make a difference in the lives of children like these."*

In that moment, I knew that I had found my calling. I reached for my journal, the place where I wrote down my deepest thoughts and aspirations, and wrote down my newfound resolve.

Connecting The Dots

During Stanford University's June 2005 commencement speech, Steve Jobs said:

> "You can't connect the dots looking forward; you can only connect them looking backwards. So you have to trust that the dots will somehow connect in your future. You have to trust in something—your gut, destiny, life, karma, whatever. This approach has never let me down, and it has made all the difference in my life."

It is only by reflecting that meaning is extracted from our life experiences. My classmate's journal, my father's heartfelt prayer and incredible journey and seeing the impact that the orphanage could have on a friend in school, created a firm impression in my heart as a little girl and that silent prayer in my room that day was answered many years later.

Now that my university study was delayed by several industrial strike actions, my life had to go on a more positive trajectory. I now wanted more out of life; more than becoming educated and getting the best grades possible, I desired to make a profound difference in my life. The dreams and visions in my heart were increasing by the day and I wanted to do everything within my power to give expression to those dreams. *Follow me in the **next chapter** as I show you the baby steps that created the massive impact you now see today.*

CHAPTER KEYPOINTS

- Dreams change, and that's okay. I wanted to become a medical doctor, but I ended up studying Botany. Life's twists can lead to the unexpected, but sometimes better, destinations.
- Imagine a 4-year plan becoming a 7-year journey. Strikes, protests—my education had its share of challenges. Yours might too, but keep pushing.
- Those dreams I had became my guide. They guided me and inspired me on this journey of impact. Your dreams might have a message too. Pay attention; they could be your compass.
- Childhood events shape our purpose. Yours have too. Pay attention to them.

Chapter **Two**

Finding My Path

"Your own path you make with every step you take. That's why it's your path."

~ Joseph Campbell

CHAPTER TWO

As a student at Lagos State University, the sight outside the campus gate was heartbreaking. Littered across the streets were men and women with their new-borns and young children, begging for alms from passers-by. All I could see were innocent kids, robbed of their childhood, and forced to endure the harsh realities of life on the streets. This sight haunted me.

It was a stark contrast between our lives as students on campus and theirs. Here was I, privileged to attend a university of higher learning, while just a few meters away, young lives were being ravaged by poverty and a lack of education. I knew I had to do something.

With a burning desire to help, I rallied a small group of like-minded friends who desired to make a difference. We scrounged together whatever resources we could find and visited orphanages, reaching out to as many families as we could.

Sometimes, we woke up before the crack of dawn to cook meals for those on the streets. The joy we felt when we saw the smiles on their faces was indescribable. We saved every penny we could, pooling our resources to feed and support these families, to at least ease their burden, even if it was just for a day.

Our efforts went unnoticed by most. We quietly carried out our mission, driven by a deep sense of purpose and compassion. But to those whose lives we touched, we were angels in human form.

The Dreams

From time to time in my dreams, I saw innocent children in helpless situations, crying and in pain. I'd see myself receiving them from their parents and cradling them in my arms, and almost immediately, their crying and pain would stop. This was just one of several.

While I studied at the university, a six-month industrial strike broke out. As I toiled through the six-month strike,

I discovered new things about myself. I, who had never considered myself a dreamer, found myself whisked away to a world where my purpose and assignment became clearer. My conviction about a future laced with impact became stronger. So vivid were my dreams that I could recall them in detail and went ahead to journal them as I remembered.

On December 10, 2005, a day that will forever be etched in my memory, Pastor Bimbo Odukoya boarded a flight that would change the course of her life. Little did she or any of us know that moments later, the aircraft would crash, and the very next day, December 11, 2005, she would bid farewell to the world. This news was unexpected and it shook the entire nation.

Until the time of her death, she was the Associate Senior Pastor of The Fountain of Life Church and the President of Discovery for Women.

She was also the host of Single and Married, a television programme broadcast locally and internationally that handled practical issues people faced in marriages and relationships. Her teachings were generally guided by biblical principles and she was a well-known conference speaker within Nigeria and internationally.

What did this have to do with me? I wasn't a member of the church or related to her in any way, but I had watched her messages repeatedly and been blessed and inspired by her life journey. She was a woman I admired and a great role model.

The day after she passed away, December 11, I had a dream where she came walking to me dressed in a white and light blue shirt and jeans to match, as she normally would wear whenever she was addressing the young audience in her church. She walked up to me in the dream with two of my friends standing on either side.

In the real sense, she didn't say any direct words at first, but it appeared we were communicating from spirit to spirit. She then asked, "Where is the money you are saving up for the orphanage?"

"Orphanage? How did she know?"

This came straight out of nowhere because I hadn't told anyone about my plans to visit the orphanage, except for a close friend. For her to have asked, God definitely wanted me to know something.

I actually planned to use the savings to purchase gifts and support materials for the children at the Heart of Gold Hospice, which is based in Surulere, Lagos.

She not only inquired about my savings but also requested that I hand over the money to her. I was hesitant, yet I knew I could trust her. I handed her the money, and as I did so, it felt as if everything I had worked so hard for was being taken away from me. It was my life's savings, after all.

She received the money from me, and for a moment, I stood there wondering what would happen next. But just as I was coming to terms with my loss, she asked me to stretch out my hands once more. Without knowing what was happening, I did. And then, from her hands, new hundred-naira notes began pouring endlessly into mine. It was a surreal experience, and I couldn't believe my eyes.

As I stood there, watching the notes pile up in my hands, I couldn't contain my shock and wonder. It was a powerful lesson in trust and faith.

This was a miracle in a sense—much more than I could ever ask, think, or even imagine.

Still in the dream, my friends and I argued back and forth about how to reach the orphanage via the telephone to inform them about our plans to visit. Just then, Pastor Bimbo brought out a phone from her pocket. The phone was made of gold and glistened like a piece of glass in the sunlight. I couldn't even stretch my hands to receive it from her. It was just too precious and radiant.

Then, a few moments later, Pastor Taiwo Odukoya, her husband, walked up to where we stood, took the phone right from her hands and placed the call on our behalf. It was then that I jolted out of sleep.

The coming of this dream also coincided with the time I was reading *'The Assignment'* by Dr. Mike Murdock.

What did this mean?

The money poured endlessly from her hands to mine. The golden phone. Pastor Taiwo Odukoya was making the call on our behalf.

Like the biblical Nebuchadnezzar, I was transfixed by the message this dream had, and sought to get an understanding.

One thing was clear: God was confirming to me that the thoughts and desires I had to help others were definitely from him and whatever resources I would require would be abundantly supplied.

It didn't end there. In another dream, Pastor Bimbo Odukoya was narrating to me how she managed her huge work and life schedule. The life balance was definitely a handful, but she had learned the wisdom to ensure her ministry and home front were well managed.

I remember walking up to her in the dream and then asking her as she walked away, "Why are you telling me all these?" She said she was only permitted to say all that she had said; anything more was not possible.

My dreams often played out like a movie. They were dramatic, but it was all preparation for the future that awaited me.

Those dreams became a lifeline, a glimmer of hope in the midst of uncertainty. They pushed me to dig deeper, to prepare myself, and to give my all to see that they became a reality. And in the end, they led me to a realisation: that I was meant for something greater than just getting a degree and settling into a career like everyone else.

One day, I shared my dreams with a pastor who often visited our campus. His response was unexpected, but it resonated with something deep inside me: "You have a calling. God is calling you to start a foundation," he said.

With newfound clarity and conviction, I set out on a journey to discover my true calling. It was a journey that would take me down unexpected paths and challenge me in ways I never thought possible.

Heading to NYSC

I was posted to ENUGU for my youth service. Not wanting to influence the decision on where to be posted, I aligned and went ahead to the NYSC Orientation Camp for the 3-week compulsory exercise. The National Youth Service Corps (NYSC) is a program created by the Nigerian government that requires all graduates under the age of 30 to serve their country for one year through various assignments, including community development projects, teaching, and other services, to promote national unity and development. Armed with a sense of purpose, I went with so much intentionality to make the most of the one-year period.

One of the plans I mapped out was to use my learned skill of bead-making as a business and to empower others to do the same. Asides teaching fellow corpers how to make beads, I also sold recharge cards.

After the camping exercise, I was posted to the outskirts of Enugu State for my PPA (Place of Primary Assignment). The town was called Eziama Amechi-Idodo. It was a village close to the borders of Ebonyi State.

Eziama Amechi Idodo, a town located in the Nkanu East Local Government Area of Enugu State, Nigeria, is one of the several towns that make up the Eziama community, which is known for its rich cultural heritage and historical significance.

The history of Amechi Idodo dates back to the pre-colonial era, when it was founded by a group of settlers who migrated from nearby communities in search of fertile land for farming. This town was surrounded by hills, valleys, lush green vegetation and numerous streams and rivers.

A friend—a staff turned family friend—of my dad's, Mr. Azubuike, picked me up from the orientation camp after the 3-week exercise and took me to the town where the place of primary assignment was located. I would later know that this town was called by some people "the forgotten village."

As we drove into the town, I could count on the top of my fingers nine different lunatics roaming about carefree, their nudity on full display. It wasn't exactly the warmest of welcomes, and I couldn't help but wonder why such a sight was my introduction to this town.

Despite my apprehension, I reminded myself that God had a purpose for me there, and that purpose would guide me to the right people and places within the town. I took a deep breath and heaved a sigh.

When we arrived, I noticed their houses were built sparsely. And they were surrounded by tall Iroko trees all around. Their only source of water was the stream. It wasn't clean, nor was it drinkable.

All in all, my safety and security were important to me and this informed my choice of accommodation. The houses I was taken to didn't have doors, and those that had doors had no locks on them. This meant anyone could walk in whenever they wanted.

I was then referred to Igwe's palace to find a place to stay. In the palace too, there were no locks on their doors. Anyone could walk in whenever they liked. I couldn't stay there either.

"With the way you are complaining about our houses here, you must be from a rich home," one of the makeshift house agents said to me on one of the house-hunting occasions.

I eventually found a suitable place and settled there.

The struggle to find a single bar of mobile network signal was all too familiar all through my service year. It was like finding a needle in a haystack. In order to get in touch with me, my contacts had to make sure they called or sent their messages to me before 4 p.m., the time when I left school for the lodge. Beyond that point, I was marooned in a sea of radio silence until I returned to the world of connectivity the next day. It was like being stranded on a deserted island, with no one to talk to but the rustling trees and the chirping birds on the roof.

I often had to take a 2-hour journey to get to the local government on the days we had our weekly meetings.

In the school I was posted to, I taught the subjects of biology and integrated science. I also had to teach the entire school these two subjects—a task that was daunting in itself. I also had to learn their language compulsorily so I could interact better.

I don't remember ever seeing the bulbs go on all through my service year, but I had a lot of help from the students who helped me get water and cleaned up my apartment whenever they had a chance.

I was only paid N500 (this is less than a dollar) but it meant the world to them, even though it was too little for anything. I made money from the products I made.

One of the members of staff mentioned that, though she loved my entrepreneurial spirit, none of my ideas could take flight.

Why? I asked. She said other corps members had tried before but failed.

I made up my mind that I would find a way to succeed despite the difficulties. This led me to begin an after-school teaching class in which I charged each of the interested students N200 because that was the amount I believed they could afford.

What a school this was! They didn't have even simple items like a school bell to notify them of changes in lesson periods.

My taking notice of the problem wasn't just for me to complain or feel like life handed me a terrible choice by being posted here; rather, it left an impression on me to find ways to ease their burden and help the students. First, I purchased a school bell for them, which they could ring at intervals to signify a change in periods.

I was later christened by the locals *"Onwa Teacher,"* translated as *"Village Teacher."*

Distraction often springs up when attempting to do great things. I found myself getting unwanted advances and marriage offers both directly and indirectly from the local men, at least the few who were a bit learned, and especially barbers and palm wine tappers. At some point, people began to insinuate that the Igwe could get married to me. I believe this was because the 60-year-old traditional ruler had married one of the serving female corps members who served a year before I came to that town. In fact, at the time I was there, she already had two children for him.

When the advances became uncomfortable for me, I began taking my security and my prayer life more seriously. I wasn't in Enugu to get married but to serve.

I was later appointed as an Area Zonal Coordinator for the NCCF Corps members in Nkanu East Local Government. NCCF stands for the Nigerian Christian Corpers' Fellowship, which is a community of Christian youths who are members of the National Youth Service Corps (NYSC) in Nigeria. They come together to worship God, serve their communities, and support one another during their service year. I began leading the fellowship with other corps members from the neighbouring villages. The neighbouring village was about a 2-hour walk away. I decided to turn this into an opportunity to have a prayer walk. It was on one of those journeys that I saw students in uniforms, and they were walking barefoot in the scorching Sun. This wasn't the first time I would see the children in this way.

On one of my prayer walks, I could hear God speak to my heart, *"You can do something about this!"*

What exactly was I going to do now?

Along the way, the thought came into my mind to help some of the students pay their fees, particularly the children who topped their classes and struggled financially. I was being paid N500 (less than a dollar) as my monthly salary by the school, and I eventually diverted the funds into helping them.

I also noticed that some of the students had torn uniforms. I used the funds to help some of them make new uniforms from a tailor that was around the school.

I also became a part of the MDG[1] projects. Specifically, I began a club and taught them a lot that related to the goals. I taught the girls how to make basic baked products

---

1 Millenium Development Goals

like chin-chin and doughnuts, so they could fend for themselves outside of school.

I had to teach the children in pidgin English. I encouraged them to think about the future.

They had little or no desire for a brighter future. Through the club, I made them realise that there's more to life than what they had around them.

I began teaching the children to make beads, as I did for my fellow youth corps members at the NYSC orientation camp.

The Big Project

I conceived an idea to provide school shoes for the students in the community primary school. This was going to cost a lot more money than I had access to. But I knew I would be able to find a way once I resolved to do it.

Raising money was difficult. The contacts I reached out to could not help. Eventually, the first sum came in. Drum rolls. A whopping sum of N1000 (just a little above $1). It was at best a seed so I kept it in the middle of my Bible.

In that same season, I attended a church service and was led to give all I had towards an urgent need. I dropped it, and I was prayed for by the pastor of the congregation. True to what the pastor said, three months later, money came in, and I raised all the money I needed.

It reminded me again of the dream where Pastor Bimbo returned to me with endless cash. I knew again that I could not lack.

I went ahead and purchased over 150 school shoes for the children. My dear friends Gbemi (who later became a member of the board of DCF), Wunmi, Ife (who is now my husband) and a few others assisted in every way they could.

We distributed the school shoes, took pictures, and documented the entire experience.

Yet on another occasion, I came across a young lady who had just gained admission and was on the verge of losing it because of her inability to pay her fees and other bills to settle on campus. I felt the need to help again.

I had a habit of saving money—the same sum I paid as my tithe. The sums I saved were often diverted into my investment portfolio. Seeing no other way, I called my stockbroker from Enugu to help me sell some shares, which would help me pay the school fees for this student. My husband, who was a friend then, helped me make the payment after receiving the funds.

As the founder of Dolly Children Foundation, I travelled to be part of the community project in Pupule village, Taraba state which was executed by the then Vice-President of the foundation, Doyin Sowunmi. This was my first time visiting the northern part of the country.

Towards the end of the service year, the LGI (Local Government Inspector for Youth Corps) members in my location asked all the corps members who had done a project to submit evidence for documentation, and others who were still on it should complete it before a set date.

When I submitted my evidence for the project, the LGI and NYSC officials were shocked and even reprimanded me for not informing them about such a huge project. I thought everything would end there, but like the scriptures say, *"She kept the sayings in her heart."*

During our passing out parade, the Enugu State Government gave me a recommendation award for my service. I was shocked because I wasn't expecting an award.

As the NYSC journey drew to a close, I intentionally began to journal about what my life would be like after this season. I began to declare and speak positively about the future that awaited me.

I also procured my first international passport during the process.

The NYSC journey helped me discover myself spiritually and intellectually and fine-tune the dream that I always had.

Weeks after my passing out, I travelled out of the country for my master's programme in the United Kingdom for a programme in Child Health & Social Care. My supervisor guided me during the course of my programme; she was a guardian angel. I also had the chance to be an assistant lecturer for her. I experienced a bit of racism, but with her help, I surmounted it all.

While in the United Kingdom, I also had the opportunity to learn how to write better and worked on different children-based projects. It used to be a herculean task, but it became a bit easier for me.

The path to seeing the fulfilment of the dreams in our hearts often comes through many events. Not one. Each one is tilting us, leading us to the exact place that has been assigned to us in destiny. In the next chapter, we explore some of the challenges with educational development in our nation.

CHAPTER KEYPOINTS

- There is no one way to find your path in life. As our faces are different, so are our paths. As long as the burning desire remains within us, we will find exactly what we ought to do.
- I have learned that help will be made available to me always for every assignment I have on my hands.

Chapter **Three**

Challenges of Education in Nigeria

"Whatever the cost of our libraries, the price is cheap compared to that of an ignorant nation."

-Walter Cronkite

CHAPTER THREE

THE SUN RISES DAILY AND SHINES IN ITS FULL STRENGTH across the length and breadth of the nation, but for many young Nigerian children, it is just another day in the struggle for education. For others, it is the consequence of a lack of it.

I find it staggering that UNESCO estimates that, as of 2022, there are over 20 million out-of-school children in Nigeria. This is nearly the entire population of Lagos State and even the population of entire countries like Mali, Chile, Romania and Malawi.

Imagine an entire nation where its entire population is unlearned and lacks the required skills and knowledge to compete with their peers in the world.

The literacy level of a nation points to how developed the nation would be. What's a nation without an educated elite in large numbers?

Children are the hope and future of every nation. Like John F. Kennedy once said, *"Children are the living messages we send to a time we will not see."*

This reminds me of the lyrics of Whitney Houston's song'

> "The Greatest Love of All."
>
> "I believe the children are our future
>
> Teach them well and let them lead the way
>
> Show them all the beauty they possess inside
>
> Give them a sense of pride to make it easier
>
> Let the children's laughter remind us how we used to be. "

Our children are, indeed, our future. They hold within them the potential to change the world, but this potential can only be realised with proper education. Unfortunately, in Nigeria, many children are denied this fundamental right.

In many parts of the country, the lack of basic educational infrastructure is shocking, to say the least. The majority of the schools in the metropolis or urban areas get better attention in terms of support from the government and corporate organisations than the ones in remote or rural areas and those on the outskirts.

We see the sorry state of children without desks and chairs writing on the bare ground and in classrooms where their roofs may even be non-existent. This situation is worsened by the lack of political will by the government to prioritize education.

As a result, many children are left to fend for themselves. Due to poverty, many children at the grassroots are compelled to work as economic tools to add to their family income. They resort to selling on the streets or engaging in menial jobs just to make ends meet. Education, which should be a means of empowerment, becomes a luxury that only a few can afford.

The consequences of a society where its youth are not properly educated are severe. We see its effect in young men smashing the windscreens of vehicles with the intent to steal and cause harm to commuters who may be stuck in traffic jams. We see the effect of able-bodied young men deployed as thugs during election cycles. We see it in young boys and girls engaging in fraud and prostitution to live up to the standards they might have seen in the media. Poverty, an increase in crime rates, and insecurity are a few of the effects of a society that does not prioritise quality education.

In a country as rich in human and natural resources as Nigeria, we should not suffer this fate. More investment needs to be made.

Our children are the future, and the foundation of every great society lies in their education. Unfortunately, in Nigeria, this foundation is being shaken to its core. The educational system is plagued with infrastructural decay, teacher negligence, and appalling conditions of service. It's a grim reality, but we refuse to accept that this is the best we can do for our children!

The government has implemented policies aimed at reducing street begging and boosting school enrollment, but these policies are not enough. Shockingly, a recent UNESCO report revealed that around 20 million children still cannot attend school due to poverty and financial constraints.

We cannot stand by idly and watch the next generation suffer like this. Our team experienced the devastating consequences of this issue firsthand during our summer school project two years ago. More than 60% of the children who attended had not received a formal education in four years! We must take decisive action to prevent long-term negative effects, such as a rise in poverty, unemployment, child marriage, teenage pregnancy, and a host of other social and economic problems.

It's time for the government to act fast and prevent this ticking time bomb from exploding and ruining the country's future. We cannot let the lack of education for millions of Nigerian children lead to more systemic problems such as increased security challenges, corruption, gender inequality, and a bad international reputation (Chinwumba and Ayoka, 2022).

What's wrong with education in Nigeria?

At this point, many would ask what has gone wrong with the education system in Nigeria. There is no one-size-fits-all answer to this. They include the increase in examination malpractice, poor access to funding, religious bias, inadequate facilities for teaching, and poor teacher training and motivation, amongst others. As a practitioner in this field, I've come across these challenges more times than I can count.

Each of these factors in themselves is strong enough to reduce the quality of education children receive, but the combined challenges make it even tougher. These factors impede productivity on different levels: the teacher side and the student side. These challenges, without a doubt, have constantly fueled the desire of students to transit out of the country in search of better educational and job opportunities.

Education is an investment that pays the best interest. I saw it first in the life of my dad, and now mine, and in the lives of several thousands of students that our foundation has been able to change over its almost two decades of existence.

We may have a long road to travel to create the kind of educational system we desire as a country, but commendable is the fact that most parents are eager to send their children to school. Being educated gives children a better chance at success in life. If the government and private investors can invest more in the education sector by providing better facilities, decent teachers' salaries and welfare, increasing funding for the education sector, including the inclusion of new topics in the curriculum, tackling the issue of examination malpractice, etc., the standard of education in Nigeria can be improved. This will not only benefit the country but also the students and the entire society.

I'll attempt to discuss a few of the salient challenges and a few solutions.

Poor Reading Culture

There is a popular quote which says that if you want to hide something from a black man, put it in a book. This statement may sound like a joke, but it is a harsh reality. Books are a source of knowledge and information that can help children achieve their goals and make the right decisions. Unfortunately, a significant number of Nigerian children and adults have a poor reading culture. A key factor causing this is distraction.

A significant portion of this distraction is casued by the excessive and unguarded use of social media, cable television/ streaming platforms, and video games. These distractions make it difficult for them to develop an interest in reading. They would rather spend their time on these entertaining activitieis than read a book.

Unfortunately, this trend continues throughout their education, leading to poor academic performance and a lack of desire to pursue knowledge. In addition to this, there is also the challenge of a lack of access to quality education materials, such as textbooks and reading materials.

Most schools—especially public schools—do not have libraries or provide their students with relevant materials for their studies. Of course, this will further discourage reading and the cycle continues.

A quick search of the number of available libraries in the United States compared to Nigeria reveals a staggering difference. According to the American Library Association, there are an estimated 117,341 libraries of all kinds in the United States today. In addition, there are also numerous academic and research libraries, as well as a large number of private libraries. However, in Nigeria, the case is different.

There are 43 libraries established in federal universities, 48 libraries founded in state-owned universities and 79 libraries founded in private universities.

A 2014 report by the Nigerian Library Association estimated that there were only about 100 public libraries in the country, with many of them filled with outdated materials and dilapidated infrastructure.

The consequences of a poor reading culture are huge. Poor reading skills lead to a lack of comprehension, which affects academic performance and even future career prospects. It also limits the ability to think critically and makes it difficult to make informed decisions. As a result, the country's development is slowed down, and the citizens are unable to compete on a global scale.

To address this challenge, the government and stakeholders in the education sector must prioritise the development of a reading culture in Nigeria. Schools must have well-equipped libraries and provide students with access to quality textbooks and reading materials. Parents must also encourage their children to read by setting an example and providing an environment conducive to reading. Reading competitions, book clubs, and literary events should also be organised to promote reading and literacy among students. This is one of the programmes we run so as to address the illiteracy culture.

Lack of Proper Data on Education-Related Issues

As much as poor reading culture is a major challenge to education in Nigeria, poor data availability is another key obstacle to educational development in the country.

Imagine a young student, Chidi, who wants to write a research paper on the effects of climate change on agriculture in Nigeria. He goes to the library at his school, hoping to find relevant books and articles to use for his research. To his disappointment, he finds only a few outdated books and articles that are no longer relevant or accurate.

Chidi decides to search online for more information, but he quickly discovers that many of the online resources are inaccessible due to poor internet connectivity and high data costs. Even when he manages to access some of the resources, he realises that much of the data is either inaccurate or unreliable.

Chidi's experience is not unique. In fact, it is common for students and researchers in Nigeria to face significant challenges accessing accurate and reliable data. This is due to a number of factors, including poor infrastructure, inadequate funding, and limited capacity for data collection and management.

Without access to accurate data, it is difficult for students and researchers to conduct meaningful research and produce high-quality work.

Without reliable data, it is difficult to correctly assess the state of education in the country, identify areas that need improvement, and allocate resources appropriately.

Maybe the reason education isn't properly funded is due to incorrect data available to decision making in government. This lack of funding goes on to affect others aspects of the education sector.

To address this challenge, the Nigerian government has to prioritise investment in data collection, management, and dissemination. This includes improving infrastructure, increasing funding, and building capacity for data collection and analysis. Only then can Nigeria fully harness the power of data to drive educational development and achieve its full potential.

Conclusion

As we come to the end of this chapter, it's time for us to take action! The future of education in Nigeria is at stake, and it's up to all of us to do our part in creating a better tomorrow. Parents, teachers, government officials, and other stakeholders, it's time to step up and take charge.

Let's put an end to the poor reading culture and lack of access to quality education that's been holding our children back. We must invest in our schools, provide resources and training for our teachers, and create a system that nurtures the talents and potential of our students. We have the power to make a difference, but we must act now. The time to transform education in Nigeria is now.

In the next chapter, I'll take you on a journey of the growth of the Dolly Children Foundation...

CHAPTER KEYPOINTS

- Education shouldn't depend on where you live. Kids scribbling on the ground due to a lack of desks is a serious reminder of the uneven opportunities in Nigeria.
- Poverty shouldn't steal childhoods. Many kids are forced to work to survive, and therefore they miss out on education. It's a struggle against the odds, and we need to change this narrative.
- The chaos in the classrooms, decay, and teacher neglect are alarming. We can't turn a blind eye to a broken educational system that jeopardizes the future of our children.
- Policies to curb street begging and boost enrollment aren't enough. Poverty still keeps around 20 million kids away from school. The government needs a better game plan.
- We do not just have an education crisis on our hands; it's a ticking time bomb. Without urgent action, we risk a future marred by deeper issues.

Chapter **Four**

Launching Dolly Children Foundation

"Take the first step in faith. You don't have to see the whole staircase, just take the first step."

- Martin Luther King Jr.

CHAPTER FOUR

When my pastor confirmed that God really would have me open a foundation, I took it to heart. But where was I going to start? Opening a foundation seemed like a huge mountain that I needed to surmount. I decided to start by picking up the building blocks; i.e., getting the right information.

The internet was still in its infancy in Nigeria, and mobile phones were just starting to gain internet access. I mainly relied on cybercafés to get online. I would search for information on how to start an NGO in Nigeria and similar topics.

Most of the available information at that time was focused on NGOs abroad. There was very little guidance on how to start a foundation in Nigeria.

I did most of my research online, learning about CAC[2] registration from others and setting aside weekly time to continue my exploration. I discovered that many foundations began with someone's personal story or a burning desire to solve a problem, ultimately changing lives in their communities. Even though I didn't find much information on NGOs in Nigeria, the stories of international NGOs greatly inspired me.

I had a strong desire to replicate the success stories of international NGOs in Nigeria. Engaging in charity work became my passion. I would use the pocket money my dad gave me as a student to buy GCE[3] forms for others. This cause was close to my heart because I, too, had struggled with GCE exams and had to write them three times before finally achieving the results I needed. Eventually, I passed the International GCE, obtaining all the required papers at once.

Given that I had received divine instruction to start an NGO, I knew I had to take the plunge. I connected with a lawyer and another individual who could provide the

---

2. Corporate Affairs Commission

3 General Certificate Examinations

necessary information for starting one in Nigeria. My friend Bukola was also a great help throughout the process.

In the midst of my passionate endeavours, little did I know that the eyes of others were keenly observing my every move. It was during this time that my dear friend, Bukola, became inspired to embark on her own charitable initiatives. However, she hesitated, feeling that she lacked the necessary resources to make a significant impact. I reassured her that she didn't have to wait for a fortune to make a difference. I emphasised that helping others is not about the size of your bank account but about the compassion in your heart. When your heart is filled with a genuine desire to give, resources have a way of finding their way into your hands.

Following this conversation, I shared with Bukola the project I had been planning—an upcoming visit to an orphanage. I had been diligently saving funds for this venture, and I had also been collecting gifts that were graciously bestowed upon me. When Bukola heard about my project, her interest soared, and she decided to join forces with me.

As the next semester began, Bukola contributed N5,000 in support of our project. Her commitment mirrored my own, and I was truly grateful. Unfortunately, it was during this semester that I fell seriously ill—a debilitating illness that impacted my overall well-being. Despite valiant efforts and a constant stream of medication, my health continued to decline. Since I was studying in Lagos, I also resided with my aunt who also was based in Lagos at the time. The school nurse didn't seem to grasp the severity of my suffering too.

Three agonizing days passed with me bedridden, unable to even stand. Worried, my aunt and uncle rushed me to a nearby hospital. I received an injection, but to my horror, a lump formed at the injection site. Despite raising concerns, the dismissive nurse assured them it was normal and would disappear. She applied ice which gave me temporary relief, but I wanted to be well.

As I got better, I returned to school, but then, something very disturbing began to happen to me. Every time I sat down, my seat became damp. The unnerving phenomenon didn't escape my classmates, who brought it to my attention This was too obvious that my coursemates also called my attention to it.

These events coincided with the preparations for the launch of the foundation and the project I was carrying out with Bukola. Despite these setbacks, I knew I couldn't abandon my plans. I turned to prayer, and sought God for divine healing. They say encouragement is oxygen to the soul, I'm glad I had this during this period. A friend shared with me a message she received from God. Her message was simply to urge me to keep on firing on the journey of vision I was already on. Oh, was I now more fired up.

Miraculously, God answered my prayers, and my healing unfolded rapidly. I diligently took my antibiotics, and within a week, everything cleared. It was truly a testament to the power of faith and resilience.

Finally, the day arrived when I visited the Heart of Gold orphanage—an organisation I had discovered online. This particular orphanage provided care for children facing various health challenges, including hydrocephalus and other conditions. Armed with gifts and the funds I had diligently saved, I had the privilege of meeting the founder. In the midst of our interaction, I sensed her inspiration and curiosity. Intrigued by my petite stature, she inquired about the motivations behind my project. Captivated by her genuine interest, I poured out my heart, recounting the vivid dreams I had experienced and the divine instruction I had received to establish a foundation. Her encouragement resonated deeply within me, further fuelling my determination on this remarkable journey.

Back at school, I continued to share my dreams with my peers, gathering under the sheltering branches of a tree behind the Faculty of Science building, LASU. These meetings became pivotal as we collectively crafted the vision, mission, and code of conduct for the foundation. As I shared my vision, my friend Bunmi skilfully translated it into a captivating logo. The first logo featured a plant, symbolising my profound love for both nature and children. With each meeting, we felt our spirits soar, inching ever closer to the realisation of our heartfelt mission.

And so it began. In 2006, we launched unofficially, starting with food and clothing outreaches to communities in need. We taught children to read and write, visiting public schools, orphanages and donating writing materials. We spoke to them about the power of education and the difference it could make in their lives.

For five years, we did what we could, but it wasn't enough. We knew we had to focus on what really made a difference. So, we picked one programme, the one with the greatest impact, and we zeroed in on it, putting everything else in the background. And that's when the real magic began.

Why we started with Primary Education

While growing up, I knew that children often dropped out of secondary school, but after returning from the UK to Nigeria, reality hit me hard. I discovered that even primary school children were affected by this problem.

I became even more concerned when I realised there were statistics supporting this too. This compelled me and my team to focus on helping these young learners, particularly those at the primary level.

With a clear goal in mind, we set out to design and implement programmes that would prevent children from dropping out and ensure they stayed in school. We wanted to track those at risk of abandoning their education and provide them with the support they needed to continue their academic journey.

Our mission was to empower these children and show them the immense value of education. We believed that every child, regardless of their circumstances, deserved a chance to dream and succeed. So, we poured our passion and dedication into developing comprehensive initiatives that addressed the challenges they faced.

It wasn't an easy task, but our determination never wavered. We knew that we needed to take action and make a tangible impact. The statistics served as a constant reminder of how important and urgent the mission of the Dolly Children Foundation was, motivating us to push forward and break the cycle of this challenge in the lives of kids.

We knew that by addressing the root causes and providing proactive support, we could make a difference in the lives of these children. We were driven by the belief that education is a powerful tool for empowerment and a gateway to a better future.

Despite the challenges we faced, we remained steadfast. We understood that the journey would be tough, but the impact we could make was immeasurable. Every child we reached, and every life we touched, became a testament to the power of our efforts.

Looking back on our humble beginnings, we stand tall, knowing that we have changed lives and instilled hope in the hearts of those we serve. Our dedication to school children starting from the primary level has continued to wax strong. I believe that every child deserves a quality education.

Our work is far from complete, but we continue to march forward, driven by the belief that no child should be left behind.

With each step we take, we are shaping a brighter tomorrow, one child at a time. Education is the key that unlocks endless possibilities, and we are committed to ensuring that every child has the opportunity to thrive and succeed.

CHAPTER KEYPOINTS

- Starting the foundation seemed as difficult as climbing a mountain, but the journey began with online searches and dreaming big. It's a reminder that every grand mission starts with a humble search for knowledge and answers.
- You don't need a fortune to make a difference. Compassion trumps bank account size. It's a call to action: help with what you have, where you are.
- Miracles happen when determination meets faith.
- We didn't start this foundation in the board room, but under a tree. This proves that impactful ideas don't always need fancy settings. Magic always happens when passionate and committed people team up to do great things.
- Focus is necessary to create a difference in whatever you do.

Hearts and Hands

Chapter **Five**

The Work and Life Balance

"Never get so busy
making a living that
you forget to make a
life."

– Dolly Parton

CHAPTER FIVE

LOVE HAS A WAY OF SHAPING THE COURSE OF OUR LIVES. AS I embarked on my journey to make a difference, little did I know that love would not only accompany me but become an inseparable part of my vision.

After my NYSC, I knew I was going to further my studies abroad, and this decision will affect every other aspect of my life. Around that same time, I had accepted a relationship proposal from my now husband, but the thought of travelling made me question the future of the relationship. I didn't want to be at the centre of another *Japa*[4] love story that went sour. I was determined not to contribute to these

---

[4] A slang popular in Nigeria, West Africa, which means travelling out to other developed countries in the bid to escape the difficulties in the nation.

sad statistics, so I approached him with a heavy heart to let him know what I thought.

So, I told him one afternoon, "I know we've started this relationship already, and I said yes, but as it is now, can you just take it that I actually said NO? We can still be friends." With a mix of surprise and concern, he looked into my eyes, trying to process what I just said.

But instead of accepting defeat, he held my hands and reassured me. He said we would build a system of regular communication. Relationships are built on open and honest communication, and that is what we agreed to do. At that moment, I knew this was the right thing to do. We were going to make it work and ours will not be another love tale gone sour.

And so, our journey continued. As I pursued my studies abroad, I didn't feel pressured, we took it one day at a time. The distance was not a barrier for us, thanks to technology. With each passing week, our communication grew stronger, bridging the miles between us. Despite the distance, he made the effort to visit me there in the UK. When he came, he also met my Pastor and other people I had met during the course of my studies.

When I eventually completed my program, I secured a position, briefly, as an Assistant Lecturer at the same educational institution. But I returned to Nigeria much later, ready to embark on a new chapter both personally (to get married) and professionally (to continue the impactful work of Dolly Children Foundation). The pieces were falling into place, and our love story was entering a new phase.

Where did it all start?

It all began during our NYSC days. When I met him, he was also a serving youth corps member, and after a while, we worked on a number of projects together. He was a member of my team, and with time, I realised I could count on him when it mattered the most. I think it's a thing with ladies, we just know when a guy is into us and may ask us out.

I had known that he would eventually ask me out, so I fervently prayed for guidance on whether it was the right thing to do and the right time too. From the very beginning, he supported my aspirations and shared my vision for making a positive impact. When his request came, it didn't take long for me to give him an affirmative YES!

How we do life today

The dance of work life and personal life can be challenging, especially for me. I can say it is the same for most women as well. People often marvel at our (my husband and I) ability to maintain a stress-free work-life balance, and the answer lies in the foundation we have built. Our understanding has matured, our communication has deepened, and our love has blossomed too.

In the realm of my work, where passion and dedication are needed, having a strong support system is non-negotiable. And I am fortunate enough to find that support in my husband. Together, we have shared the responsibility of raising our children, seamlessly moving between our professional pursuits and the joys of family life.

Through the highs and lows, the challenges and triumphs, our marriage has come full circle. As I have continued to make a difference with the foundation, his unwavering presence reminds me that love, in all its forms, makes life worth living.

Gifts and more impact

One particular aspect that brings great joy to both the children and me is the tradition of giving cakes. It all began in 2015, when my husband and I decided to brighten the lives of these young students. The excitement they show is indescribable. I can't even begin to count the number of cakes we've handed out over the years. It has become a symbol of celebration, a sweet treat that signifies a moment of happiness.

Though we celebrated the results we already had, we realised that our impact had to extend beyond secondary school dropouts. I discovered that even primary school children were dropping out of school and needed urgent help. It was a wake-up call that meant I had to focus on this vulnerable age group.

I can say for a fact that the journey hasn't been without its surprises and twists too. Today, the kids call me "Auntie Dolly." It is heart-warming to see the children's excitement when they see me. They recognize me even in the hustle and bustle of the community, whether I am in a car or on a bike. Their innocent curiosity fills my heart with joy. And it isn't just the children; even the community stakeholders, the ones who see and support our efforts. This, and more, is a testament to the impact we are making, a silent recognition of the love and care we have poured into our work.

An unforgettable encounter

In the course of my work, I met a boy who I couldn't shake off my mind. He worked as a vulcanizer, and he was far too young to shoulder such responsibilities. He had to do this to make ends meet and to deal with matters that were beyond his control. I made it my mission to help him. Despite the challenges he faced, I saw a ray of hope in his eyes.

We enrolled him in school to further his education. I wish I could tell you that it was easy. It wasn't a smooth journey. We had to place him in a lower grade than his age would suggest. He was placed in Primary 2 even though he was 13 years old.

Thankfully, our efforts did not go unnoticed. An NGO that works with children living with sickle cell disease partnered with us. The RCCG[5], My Father's House Salford, Flourish Roots Foundation, and GAMSU[6] became invaluable partners in our mission. Their contributions, whether through monthly donations or book supplies, helped us bring a glimmer of hope to him and others like him.

The place of self-care

In the middle of all the impact and activities we're involved in, I prioritise self-care. I have realised the importance of finding moments of relaxation and inspiration. I often seek rest and relaxation by watching inspiring movies. In movies like "Courageous" and "Overcomers," I've found stories that continue to inspire me to be more. They remind me that even amidst the challenges, there is beauty and strength to be found.

---

5 The Redeemed Christian Church of God
6 Gamaliel & Susan Onosode Foundation

But striking a balance is no easy feat. As an NGO founder, I am always on call, ready to serve and make a difference. Yet, I have also learned the importance of self-care. Moments of reflection and retreat have become crucial, allowing me to recharge and evaluate my efforts. It is in these moments that I find clarity and inspiration, enabling me to push forward and continue impacting the lives of these children.

CHAPTER KEYPOINTS

- You can't separate love from life. It's what makes life beautiful. Love can shape not just your personal happiness but also your vision. So, choose right.
- Love knows no distance.
- For relationships to thrive, you need a strong foundation, understanding, and communication.
- Sometimes, it's the simple gestures that create profound joy. It can leave a lasting impression on others.

Chapter **Six**

The Art of Intentional Giving

"We make a living by what we get. We make a life by what we give."

- Winston Churchill

CHAPTER SIX

I N THE AFRICAN CONTEXT, THERE HAS BEEN A NOTABLE SHIFT towards more active engagement in charitable work and social causes. NGOs are sprouting up, people are stepping forward to contribute, and charity seems to be on the rise. But this is not without its challenges. The way we give matters more than what we give.

I remember attending an event where TY Bello - the Nigerian talented photographer and artiste- shared her unique perspective on her craft and how she constantly portrayed joy over suffering. TY Bello believed that presenting a smiling child in her artwork would draw people in, prompting them to inquire about the story behind the picture. By doing so, she raises awareness of the child's needs and receives support. Her words resonated deeply with me.

It dawned on me that the effectiveness of our charity work also depended on the quality and intention behind it. It's not just about collecting clothes from well-meaning donors; it's about ensuring that what we receive is far from mere cast-offs.

I remember the disappointment of seeing clothes donated by some people years ago. While these people were wealthy and comfortable, they didn't allow this to show in their giving. Rather, the clothes they donated had worn-out zippers and were in very terrible conditions. I was left wondering how someone living comfortably could offer such items as a donation; this, to me, suggested a lack of respect for the recipients.

One incident solidified my commitment to maintaining high standards. I recall a well-meaning supporter who proposed providing substandard materials to the children we serve. I responded with conviction, emphasising that we set a high standard for our intentions. We don't simply purchase anything; we believe in offering quality. This principle applies to all aspects of our foundation's work.

In our free training school, where we prepare underprivileged children for a brighter future, we hold ourselves to the highest standards. Our dedication to quality has not gone unnoticed. Friends who had only seen our work through social media were astounded by the beautiful environment we had created for these children. Their amazement stemmed from the intentionality behind every decision we made. The same teachers who worked in affluent schools chose to dedicate their time to our mission because they recognised our commitment to providing quality education and support.

Our focus on intentionality extends beyond education. We ensure that children have complete and functional clothing, and we've provided them with essential items like water bottles and bags.

I encourage all who share our passion for change to be intentional. Whether you aspire to bring transformation to the lives of children or pursue any other meaningful endeavour, intentionality is key. It manifests in the resources and effort you invest and is reflected in your preparations.

As a foundation we are intentional about how we carry out our mission. The same commitment to quality is echoed in our foundation. We never settle for less.

Here are some practical steps to practicing intentional giving:

- *Intentional giving is not about the size of the gift, but the heart behind it.* It's about making a deliberate choice to create a positive change in the lives of those in need. For me, it all started with a desire to make a difference, to extend a helping hand, and to uplift the less fortunate. The first step in intentional giving is to identify your passion and the cause that resonates with you. It could be education, healthcare, hunger, relief, or any other area where you feel compelled to make an impact. Once you've found your cause, research it thoroughly to understand the specific needs and challenges. This knowledge will guide your giving and ensure it's effective.

- *Setting clear goals is another essential aspect of intentional giving.* Determine what you want to achieve with your contributions. Are you aiming to provide clean water to a village, sponsor a child's education, or support a local shelter? Having specific objectives allows you to measure the impact of your giving and track the progress you're making. Moreover, intentional giving involves making a plan. Outline how you intend to support your chosen cause. Consider both financial contributions and non-monetary assistance, such as volunteering your time or expertise. Create a budget for your giving to ensure it aligns with your financial capacity.

- *One key element of intentional giving is ensuring that your contributions are well-directed.* Seek out reputable organisations, nonprofits, or local initiatives that are known for their transparency and effectiveness. Don't hesitate to ask questions, request information on their projects, and evaluate their track record.

- *Sharing your story and inspiring others is an integral part of intentional giving.* By sharing your experiences and the impact of your contributions, you can motivate others to join your cause. When we come together, our collective impact grows, and we can achieve more than we ever thought possible.

- Above all, *intentional giving requires ongoing commitment.* The needs of those we seek to help do not disappear after a single donation. Stay engaged with the cause you're passionate about, continue to learn, and adapt your giving strategy as circumstances evolve.

In my own journey of intentional giving, I've experienced the joy of seeing lives transformed, communities uplifted, and hope rekindled. It's a profoundly rewarding art that has enriched my life in ways I never imagined.

The art of intentional giving is not only about making a difference in the lives of others; it's about transforming our own lives through purposeful, heartfelt actions.

CHAPTER KEYPOINTS

- It's not just about what we give but also how we present it.
- Charity isn't about discarding unwanted items but about respecting the dignity of recipients.
- A commitment to excellence attracts valuable people to you.
- Embrace intentionality in all your endeavours.
- Learn from those who go beyond the basics and never settle for less.

Hearts and Hands

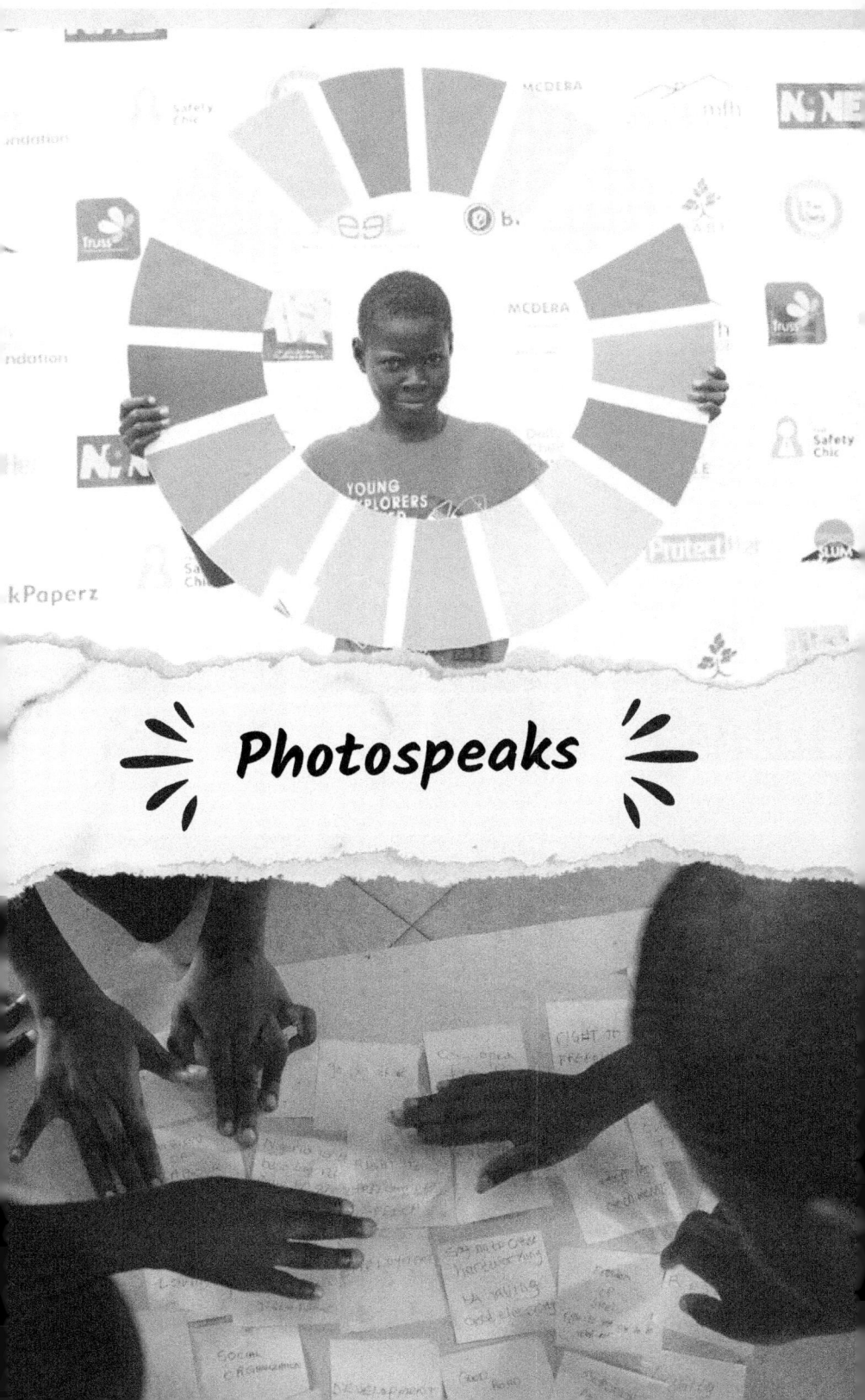

Photospeaks

Overview Of Impact

10,526
Children supported via our educational aid and welfare initiatives

23,570
Total number of children reached

29
Communities reached so far

10,460
Children that benefitted from our reading clubs

2500
Teachers trained via our teachers training programmes

48
Partnering Organizations

Chapter **Seven**

The Hands That Help and Lift

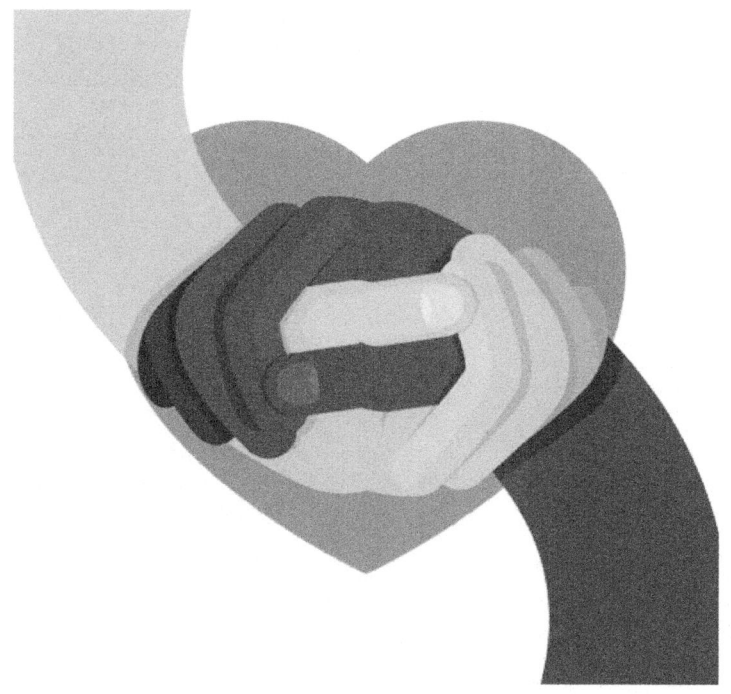

"There is no exercise better for the heart than reaching down and lifting people up."

- John Holmes

CHAPTER SEVEN

Starting a vision isn't a solo journey. While it often kicks off with one person's passion—typically the visionary—making a lasting impact requires a team effort. There's a saying that goes, **"It takes a village to raise a child,"** and I firmly believe the same applies to any significant endeavour we undertake in life. You need a community of dedicated individuals, both men and women, who share the passion, possess skills, and are committed to turning that vision into reality.

The story of the Dolly Children Foundation remains incomplete without acknowledging the intentional efforts, sacrifices, and steadfast diligence of the remarkable individuals I've encountered over the past two decades.

This 'village' is the driving force that breathed life into the dream residing in my heart.

This chapter is a heartfelt dedication to sharing their unique stories: each person who played and continues to play a crucial role in shaping and advancing the mission of the foundation.

How did you come in contact with the founder/foundation/school?

Dolapo and I have been friends for three decades. We met as fresh-faced high schoolers at Baptist Girls College. Despite her persistent efforts, I initially resisted friendship. Yet, Dolapo never wavered. While in boarding school, she always had extras to help others with. From uniforms, food, etc., each day her kindness chipped away at my walls.

Finally, I realised my mistake and became more open to her show of love and care. That was when our true bond began.

Dolapo's belief in me has been a constant for many years now. She doesn't give up on people.

Together, we established the Dolly Children Foundation in 2006. My role evolved from vice-president to managing the foundation during her Master's program.

Dolapo, a force to be reckoned with, knew her path early. She pursued her Master's program in the UK with a clear vision, even amidst societal pressures. Her supportive husband also played a major role.

Dolapo, my "younger sister" by a day, is more than a friend; she's family. Thirty years later, our bond remains strong.

What significant experiences or impacts have you witnessed so far from the school and foundation?

I'm not surprised by the great results Dolly Children Foundation has today; I saw it coming. I'm genuinely proud of the woman Dolapo has become. Reflecting on our early days post-univerity, a memory resurfaces. We, the seven members of the executive team, were tasked with writing our departmental reports. Six ladies, one guy (Seun), each with designated roles and monthly reports in tow. The details are hazy, but Dolapo made us stand and deliver. We were in our 20s, yet there we were, presenting reports on a panel. There was this unspoken fear of Dolapo—you had to be on your game. She'd give you that look, and you knew you better have your report sorted.

Leadership oozed from her every pore, even back then. People older than her willingly teamed up, drawn to her magnetic aura. Dolapo had a way of assisting without overshadowing. Working with her meant hitting your targets—there was no room for slacking off with Dolapo around.

We wrote reports and held vigils pretty frequently at the time. I remember Dolapo planning vigils, and we would go to Canaan Land. We were young then, and we were planning big events. We would bring funds together; we used to have monthly contributions; we used to go to Canaan Land and rent a flat; and we were always working on a new budget at all times. But looking back then and now, it really took strong leadership, and that is who Dolapo is.

What significant experiences or impact have you witnessed so far from the school and foundation?

The impact of the Dolly Children Foundation is nothing short of remarkable. I stumbled upon a video recently showcasing their efforts – distributing essentials like food, clothing, and more, bringing smiles to countless faces. Watching it unfold, I couldn't help but think: If more organisations like the Dolly Children Foundation exist in Nigeria, the ripple effect would be incredible. It's a game-changer, a ray of hope for those in need, showing that positive change can happen without solely relying on the government.

Imagine if the government could partner with credible NGOs like the Dolly Children Foundation, channelling funds to organisations that are making a tangible difference. It could be a key step in taking people off the streets and providing them with the means to lead reasonably comfortable lives. Dolly Children Foundation, in this regard, stands out as a highly reputable organisation.

So, if you happen to know someone with the means and the desire to make a difference, I'd say reaching out to the Dolly Children Foundation is a fantastic move. Your support could be a catalyst for positive change in the lives of many.

She's the twin sister I never had—that unbreakable bond that transcends physical distance.

Here's to more accomplishments in the name of Jesus.

God bless you, Adedolapo.

Oladoyin Sowunmi

How did you come in contact with the founder/foundation/school?

I met Dolapo Osuntuyi, the founder of Dolly Children Foundation, while taking a social sector management course at Enterprise Development Centre; she was my accountability partner, and we have been accountable to one another ever since. When I think about it and reflect on our relationship, I realise it's as if I've known her forever and the foundation.

Throughout our relationship, Dolapo and I have studied and worked together to enhance the lives of children, particularly the Dolly Children Foundation. The Dolly Children Foundation became a beneficiary of the Gamaliel and Susan Onosode Foundation, and in the last three years, GAMSU[7] has provided funding in the form of school bags, books, laptops, and pens for the children who enjoy the opportunity of being a part of the Dolly Children Foundation summer programme. I know for a fact that it has impacted over four thousand children.

My friendship with her has survived simply because she is a wonderful person. I don't think I've met anyone as passionate as she is about having children (the less fortunate) in mind. She is very passionate about what she does, and it's not just about being passionate. Dolapo is very consistent

---
7 Gamaliel & Susan Onosode Foundation

when it comes to collaboration; she collaborates with right-minded people, people who have the same target and the same vision, and that has worked well for her, which is why this relationship is still going strong. I've known her personally and as the founder of the Dolly Children Foundation, and this has endeared me to her.

What significant experiences or impact have you witnessed so far from the school and foundation?

Talking about the impact Dolapo and her foundation have had is nothing short of amazing. Every day, it hits me how significant the contribution has been. Imagine waking up and realising that there are kids out there who would typically dread summer because they'd be stuck hawking or just trying to make ends meet. Now, thanks to Dolapo, a ten-year-old can actually look forward to going to school. Even if she has to start from scratch, there's someone who cares about her school fees and her meals.

The ripple effect of Dolapo's efforts has been tremendous. It's not just about education; it's about changing the trajectory of these kids' lives. Knowing Dolapo and being a part of the foundation has been an absolute pleasure. It's not just a charity; it's a force for good, making a real, tangible difference in the lives of those who need it most.

Toyin Olanrewaju
CEO, Toyin Olanrewaju Consult

How did you come in contact with the founder/foundation/school?

The Dolly Children Foundation was founded by Adedolapo Osuntuyi, a visionary individual who saw the potential in every child and wanted to provide them with the best opportunities to succeed. The foundation journey began when Adedolapo and some of us in the university witnessed the hardship faced by the under-privilege children in our community. We felt a strong urge to help these children, who lacked food, learning materials and support.

Dolapo Osuntuyi spearheaded these initiatives and realised that education was the key to breaking the cycle of poverty and empowering these children to pursue their dreams. What began as a small initiative soon grew into this formal organisation, "the Dolly Children Foundation." This was the start of an amazing journey, one that continues to touch the lives of countless children. The foundation's greatest achievement is the establishment of a free school, a place where children from poor homes could access quality education. This school is a reflection of the foundation's dedication to providing equal education for all, regardless of their circumstances. At this school, children are not only taught academic subjects but also nurtured with values, confidence, and the belief in their unlimited potential. The holistic approach to education goes beyond the classroom which includes vocational skills, life skills, mentorship programs, and counseling services, ensuring that each child receive the support they need to flourish.

The impact of the Dolly Children Foundation is not limited to the school premises but spreads to the whole community. Over the years, many children have benefited from the foundation, equipping them with skills and knowledge, to not only improve their own lives, but also contribute to their community.

In a world full of inequalities and challenges, the Dolly Children Foundation is still a source of hope, showing the power of compassion, education, and unwavering commitment.

Its legacy will continue to inspire many individuals and communities reminding us that even the smallest act of kindness can make a big difference in the world.

Olubunmi Akingbade
(the first secretary of Dolly Children Foundation)

How did you come in contact with the founder/foundation/school?

Mrs. Dolapo Osuntuyi and I met at Life Impact Foundation International (LIFI) an NGO where she worked as a volunteer. Dolly Children Foundation was going through a reformative process. At the time she told me about it, she was doing a few programs and reaching out to the less privileged.

I've known Dolapo Osuntuyi for approximately 10 years, and in that time, I've watched her grow, I've seen her foundation expand, and I've seen her transition into doing Dolly Children Foundation full-time and reaching out to a large number of underprivileged children.

I've been like a partner because there have been occasions when I've sponsored children, supported their education, and she's also sought my professional advice on a number of issues. So, I can say that I am fairly knowledgeable about Dolly Children Foundation, how it operates, and what goes on behind the scenes.

What significant experiences or impact have you witnessed so far from the school and foundation?

But, when it comes to impact, wow, that is something that never ceases to astonish me, because Dolly Children Foundation has made a significant difference in the lives of deserving children in Makogi, Magboro, and Ibafo and its neighbouring communities. They have accomplished so much that I am at a loss for words.

One of my favourite projects was the construction of the fence around Obafemi Owode School Primary School in Makogi. It was a large project that was pretty expensive, but it was well worth it because it encouraged children to return to school. When some of the children who had dropped out of school and the entire community saw the school's new facelift, the students not only returned to school, but also loved being within the school grounds and only left when they felt like it. They were delighted to be there. Also, the new fence of over 70 m perimeter length, signage and school gate kept touts away from the school; it fenced them out while keeping the students in. This made a significant difference in the community; there was an increase in the number of children enrolled in school, and the authorities were able to keep the children within the complex and maintain discipline, which had a significant impact on the community as a whole.

The impact of the Dolly Children Foundation on kids who've returned to school is nothing short of profound. Let me share a story that really struck a chord with me.

There was this family with four incredibly bright kids. Unfortunately, circumstances had kept them out of school for over two years. Their father, struggling to make ends meet, couldn't afford the costs, not even for a public school. So, these four youngsters were stuck at home.

With the foundation's support, they managed to get back on the academic track, starting off in a public school. Within the term of their return, these kids went from being out of the system to leading their classes. It was a heartwarming transformation. The thought that such talent and intelligence might have gone to waste without someone stepping in is touching. Without intervention, they might have abandoned formal education altogether, opting for a trade or something down the line. But, thanks to the foundation, they are not only back in school but thriving. Some of them have even transitioned to private schools.

Stories like these are the true jewels, showcasing the potential that could have slipped away if not for the timely intervention of organisations like Dolly Children Foundation. It's a testament to the impact that a helping hand can have on a child's future.

I also recall the story of one particular kid, Miracle by name; I am very connected to these stories, I know them, and so giving this kind of testimony is very personal to me. So, I recall the incident of that child, she was living with her grandmother and her brother, they had lost their parents, and they were struggling. The grandmother was struggling to keep them in school, but I remember that Dolly Children picked these children and went on to sponsor them, and you could see an improvement in their academics, even in their behaviour.

Overall, I believe Dolly Children has reached over five thousand children in that area, particularly through their back-to-school project and summer holiday lessons, which bring children from various backgrounds together during the summer to teach them not only academic skills, but also marketable skills, entrepreneurship, art and craft, and a lot more. We've seen people recycling, and we've seen success stories of children.

So Dolly Children Foundation has been useful in the community where they serve, and I must say that many of the underserved children are better off now because Dolly Children Foundation picked them up.

Damilola Odukoya
CEO of Conedge Africa Limited
Certified coach, Business management consultant and a professional mental health counselor.

How did you come in contact with the founder/foundation/school?

In July 2021, I got in touch with the foundation. Mr. Romeo approached me and asked if I would be interested in participating in a summer coaching programme at an elementary school in Makogi, Ogun State. And I agreed. And I was there. That's how my summer began with Dolly Children Foundation. The summer was amazing. It was outstanding. During the summer, I met Mrs. Dolapo and many other partners, although I was just taking basic five classes at the time. So many skill acquisition opportunities were presented to me, and it was even during that summer that I learned how to make a hair, to the glory of God.

By the end of the summer, Mr Romeo informed me that he wanted me to speak with Mrs. Dolapo, the CEO of the Dolly Children Foundation so that I could possibly work with them. To God's glory, I met Mrs. Dolapo, and she accepted me. I began working with them in September that year. I worked with them and went on field trips with Mrs Dolapo. I was also taught how to prepare an action plan. I was taught how to plan ahead of time. I learned how to create action plan and the likes. I was taught so many things that I can't even begin to list them.

What significant experiences or impact have you witnessed so far?

Being a part of the Dolly Children Foundation has opened up a whole new world for me. It's more than an organisation; it's been a transformational force that has shaped the person I am today. The foundation has left its mark on me, like an indelible brand, altering the very essence of who I've become.

Dolly Children Foundation has been my constant companion, a pillar of support that has stood by me through thick and thin. It's not just an external entity; it's a defining element of my identity.

How meaningful is the contribution the foundation/school is making?

The contribution this foundation has made isn't just in the statistics or numbers reflected on their website. It changed me too and the change was noticed by everyone around me. People see the change in my confidence, my outlook, my very way of being. It's hard for them to believe, and when they whisper "good luck," I set them straight. It's not luck; it's blessings and the impact of the Dolly Children Foundation.

They shaped my skills, yes, but more than that, they shaped me too. They showed me the power of purpose, not just in grand gestures, but in the everyday.

Like the time I was lost, pregnant, and scared. Confiding in Mrs. Dolapo, I expected judgement. Instead, she held my hand and said, "Everyone makes mistakes, girl. Pick yourself up. Dolly Children Foundation is here."

Dolly Children Foundation's impact on me is immeasurable. They unearthed strengths I never knew I had, pushed me to be better. Thank you, from the depths of my grateful heart.

This journey wasn't just about me; it was about discovering a leader within. And Dolly Children Foundation saw that leader, nurtured it, and helped me blossom.

Thank you for expanding my horizons, for the experiences, and for the growth. Words fail me, but my love and commitment never will. May blessings rain upon you.

And I learned something beautiful: volunteering isn't about expecting. It's about giving, and God opening doors. Thank you for showing me that.

Thank you, Dolly Children Foundation. You are, and always will be, my family.

Olima Blessing
Project Officer, Dolly Children Foundation & Team lead for Dolly Stars School

Mrs. Dolapo and I met in 2019 through a volunteer site where we were supposed to work on a project together. Although the project did not take place, we kept that friendship, which led to learning about her work with Dolly Children Foundation. We've worked together in various roles throughout the years, and it's been an amazing experience to witness her progress.

'Mama Dolly,' as I affectionately call her, is something else – she's incredibly focused, driven, and has this deep-rooted compassion for people, which is a rare combo. It's the kind of blend that sets her apart, creating an environment where you cannot just survive but truly thrive. I'd say she's like a guiding wing, one that not only supports you but also empowers you to take flight. I hope that paints a clear picture.

There were times, various times actually, when I found myself in a bit of a low spot, and Mama Dolly, without fail, would step in to pull me out of those places, making everything better. She's been a constant advocate for me, one of my biggest supporters, and of course, my "egbon" – my big sister, as I always fondly call her. Her impact on my life is undeniable, and I'm grateful for the wings she's given me to soar.

Her work is nothing short of extraordinary. The sheer volume of what she accomplishes is mind-blowing, and you can see it in the impact she leaves behind. It's not just numbers on a spreadsheet; it's real people, real families.

I vividly recall instances like Emmanuel's and many others she's touched. Dolapo has empowered countless women, leaving an indelible mark on their lives. Take, for instance, my visit to Magboro in 2020, or at least I believe it was then. We embarked on a project that involved training over 1,400 women, and over 200 walked away with newfound empowerment kits. Now, that's not just numbers; it's a tangible impact you can feel, touch, and see. It's not just a story; it's a transformation.

Dolapo shows up every single day, consistently making a difference in the lives of these kids. Witnessing the transformation is awe-inspiring. If we had a hundred Mama Dolly scattered across Nigeria, our progress would be more than just a concept; it would be tangible. She's not just someone I admire; she's someone I eagerly look forward to seeing the outcomes of her work.

Godwin Henry
Policy & development practitioner

How did you come in contact with the founder/foundation/school?

About three years ago, I connected with the founder through Mrs. Oshikomaya, the head teacher at Obafemi Owode Community Primary School. We were chatting, and she got the scoop on what I'm up to. That's when she mentioned a foundation I should check out, run by a certain Mrs. Dolapo. I was thrilled at the chance to meet her.

It's been nothing short of fantastic since then. Even though Mrs. Oshikomaya is no longer the head teacher. The journey with Mrs. Dolapo and the Dolly Children Foundation has been amazing – full of warmth, wonder, and love.

What significant experiences or impact have you witnessed so far with them?

Based on my experience and years with them, the foundation has been a great one. One of its missions is to improve the fate of underprivileged children in Nigeria through education.

Education has always been a source of pride for her. Seeing children who have dropped out and are not receiving the greatest education possible, she saw it as her obligation to provide them with the best education possible. And not only did she provide the best education, but she also provided quality education to the students. I've seen children thrive in a positive setting, beginning with Dolly Stars School and continuing with after-school programs and mentoring session for children in other adopted schools.

The education Dolapo provides is top-notch, not just in terms of having teachers but quality teachers who are experts in their fields, subjects, departments, and classes. Plus, there's an empowerment program for less privileged children.

How meaningful is the contribution the foundation/school is making?

The founder of Dolly Children Foundation has put in real effort, tirelessly working to tackle what I'd call illiteracy, especially in rural areas. She aims to cut down child labor, prevent child abuse, and more. In the after-school lessons, they offer a free summer coaching for the kids that includes educational activities and skill training in tie and dye, tailoring, fashion designing, fruit crafts, coding, baking, soap making, hair accessories.

The kids at the foundation aren't just getting an education; they're also taught about money. There are classes on financial literacy and leadership too. The foundation also runs a program where they recycle items. It shows how supportive they are of having a healthy environment.

The idea is to give these kids skills they can use. It keeps them busy and, down the line, could help them kickstart something of their own. The foundation wants them to take what they learn and turn it into a way to make some money. Also, a good number of the kids who benefitted from these programmes have gone ahead to establish clubs in their schools so that they give back to their immediate communities.

At the end of each summer programme, the foundation sends some of the children to different programmes to learn and also interact with other children so that they're able to learn and understand what life is all about. If these children are not allowed to venture out and see things outside of their town, they may believe they are the brightest or that life ends at home. The foundation contributes to ensuring that the children receive the finest of everything.

I recall one of the programmes that the foundation sent the children to; it was called ***Project Teach a Teen***. Here the students were able to improve their skills. They learned about cinematography and photography. They also learned how to make beads, hats, and throw pillows.

I've seen the foundation do great things, like giving out lots of school bags, shoes, uniforms, exercise books, textbooks, and writing materials to kids. It's not just about the stuff they hand out – there's been a real transformation in the lives of these children, both academically and in the overall vibe of the school.

I recently witnessed the amazing work of the foundation during the General Certificate Exam (GCE) process. They partnered with an organisation to fully fund the GCE exam fees for 20 students from Magboro Community Secondary School.

This initiative aimed to empower these students by removing the financial barrier to their academic success. The results have been remarkable: the students are flourishing, and the school itself is experiencing positive outcomes.

Abubakar Arome
Tutor, Educational Consultant

How did you come in contact with the founder or the Dolly Children Foundation?

I came in contact with Mrs. Dolapo Osuntuyi, through my friend Olorunishola Abe. Olorunishola is big on advocating for various causes, and since I've always been passionate about education, I wanted to find a platform to amplify my voice. Turns out, Olorunishola was volunteering with Dolly Children Foundation, so I asked her how I could get involved in advocating for SDG4.

She told me that Dolly Children Foundation is the perfect place for that and shared the link for the volunteer application. I was a bit slow to jump on it, and when I finally decided to apply, I realised it was either the last day or the form had closed already. I dropped a comment on their Instagram page, and to my surprise, the team responded, saying they'd open the form for me. I quickly applied, went through the incubation process, and was overjoyed to find out I got selected.

One of my first tasks was to write a report on an Instagram live session we had. Even though I was at work, I managed to join the live session and submit a report. That's how I got to know Mommy Dolly (As I fondly call her), Mrs. Dolapo, and it's been a great journey since then.

What impact have you witnessed so far?

Volunteering at Dolly Children Foundation doesn't feel like a big ask. Honestly, sometimes I feel like I'm not giving enough compared to all they've given me. They've helped me grow into a better person. The kids we help at Dolly Children Foundation taught me that you can make a difference wherever you are, one child at a time.

So, what I've picked up is that you can start small. You don't need a hundred kids from the get-go. Begin with just one child, one organisation. Pour your energy and yourself into it, and the impact can go a long way. It's a reminder that even the little things matter.

In addition to this, I'm the content manager. It's such an honour to handle this part of the foundation's operations. I also anchor book reviews and meetings which helped me become a better presenter

Giving my skills to the Dolly Children Foundation feels like they're adding more value than I'm actually contributing.

Every time I step up to do something, Mummy Dolly expresses gratitude – a simple "thank you, Temiloluwa." Her encouragement is like a boost, pushing me to do things I haven't tried before. The Dolly Children Foundation keeps you on your toes, providing a platform to showcase hidden talents or skills you didn't know you had – like me speaking right now.

Speaking of Mommy Dolly, she's not just a boss; she's a wonderful person. I really appreciate her; she's not someone I take for granted. There are times when I see all the amazing things she does, and I'm like, "Oh my God, this woman can do this much." Dolly Children Foundation has been around for about 15 years, and Mommy Dolly is still graceful and humble. It makes me want to dream big and not play small.

She inspires me because she doesn't act like she's at the top and we're down there. She connects with us on a personal level, corrects gently, and is like a mother and a friend.

The training from Dolly Children Foundation have impacted me, especially one about documentation and seizing opportunities. It's made my life better, and I'm really grateful for everything they've done for me – the relationships, the lessons in leadership, and the honor of being part of the team.

How meaningful is the contribution the foundation/school is making?

I truly believe that what the school and the foundation are doing creates a ripple effect. It starts with impacting the child, then extends to the family, the community, and eventually, it reaches the state level. When you influence the children positively, it naturally influences their families. This influence then spreads to the community, and over time, it can even impact the entire state and the country. Whether we realise it or not, what these children learn influences their families, communities, and ultimately, the nation as a whole.

Education is a powerful force for development, and it shouldn't be overlooked, especially at the grassroots level. The Dolly Children Foundation is taking on this challenge, addressing the importance of education from the ground up.

The foundation's work is far-reaching, and I have to applaud them; they are doing an excellent job, and I trust that God will continue to empower and assist them, as well as supply everything they require to develop and, you know, travel beyond borders in terms of the work they do. Amen.

Temiloluwa Okunade
Content Manager, Dolly Children Foundation

How did you come in contact with the founder and the foundation?

I came in touch with Dolly Children Foundation through Mrs. Damilola Odukoya, who handles HR. She noticed my interest in working with an NGO and my love for helping kids, especially those who need it most. So, she linked me up with the founder. One cool thing I've been part of is our yearly summer/back-to-school project. We reached over 10000 kids across different communities. We teach them various skills and have mentoring sessions, all in addition to their regular school stuff. It's been a big deal for these kids.

What significant experiences or impact have you witnessed so far?

Our input always means a lot – it brings growth. Not just for the kids but for the whole community and the foundation itself. It's like a boost for the children, showing them they can aim high in their education and be confident in all they do.

Teaming up with the founder has been awesome. She's introduced me to cool strategies and tools like journaling and handling diverse groups, especially the volunteers. I can tell she's all in, dedicated to her work, and that's something I admire and aspire to.

How meaningful is the contribution the foundation/school is making?

Working with Dolly Children Foundation has stirred changes in me. I've noticed a shift, especially in how I connect with people. The foundation has opened up opportunities to engage with different folks, broadening my skills and toolset. It's been a learning journey – researching, growing, all geared towards making things better for the kids and the foundation. Thanks!

Anuoluwapo Abraham

Project Manager For Dolly Children Foundation

I've been a Dolly Children volunteer for two years now, and looking back, it's been amazing. I've grown in so many ways. Being part of making a difference in my community is a big deal to me.

When we started, we got some training that blew my mind, especially the parts about personal branding and goal setting. I was in my final year at the time, and what I learned really helped me get ready for the future and grow as a person.

Talking about impact...

We watched a video about the founder's father and from his story, it was clear that it wasn't easy for him to acquire an education. He had to work and fight for it. This made me appreciate education more and understand that not everyone has ready access to it. Many people out there have so much potential, and education could change their lives, but they don't have easy access to it. It made me see how lucky I am, but also how much needs to be done to help kids in different communities get the education they need.

And it just opened my eyes to so many things. When I heard the impact stories in the lives of the people we're helping directly—the children, their mothers—and how their lives are being changed and transformed, and how grateful they are, it showed me that one person deciding to make a difference and being intentional about reaching children, providing education and aid to them, can really, really make a significant difference.

That little thought, that little decision, can transform the world in so many ways. I've been so inspired by being a part of Dolly Children. Every day, I'm inspired by the success stories of these children. I've had the opportunity to connect with people involved in the projects, hearing their first-hand experiences.

I've read gratitude notes from students whose lives we've impacted, and it warms my heart. It opens my heart to the fact that there's so much work to be done, and the world can be a better place if each of us, brick by brick, does our part. That's the impact and significance I can say Dolly Children has had for me. In my immediate circle, I see many friends and family members inspired by what I'm a part of.

I'm grateful for the fact that I can influence others. They keep asking me, *"What's Dolly Children? What do you guys do?"* *These questions keep coming up, and people ask, "How can I be part of this? How can I make a difference?"* It shows me that each of us, when we choose a path, stands as an ambassador to make a difference or champion the cause we've decided to pursue.

We all have an assignment; we can really make a difference. It's amazing to see the amount of work we can do in that regard.

I believe that the Dolly Children Foundation and the school is making really, really great impact. In fact, the impact can't even be quantified—they continue to make a significant contribution to society at large. People's lives are being transformed each and every day and yes, education changes the mind; it transforms the mind.

I got in touch with the Dolly Children Foundation through my friend, Temiloluwa Okunade. She posted a call for volunteers on our WhatsApp status, and I saw it. Doing a little background research into what DCF was about, I discovered that they strive to provide education to children in underserved communities. Everything about the mission and vision of Dolly Children Foundation resonated with me.

Deciding that I wanted to volunteer and be part of this moving train, I joined. What I loved most was that the founder was very accessible. She connected with every member closely. We had many internal training sessions, and that's how I got to meet her. At first, I observed from afar how she handled each training, asking us questions, making us accountable.

She would inquire about our career goals, our goals for the year, what we were doing—like a catch-up and update session. It forced me to be accountable, and I was inspired by how she leads and runs the organisation.

Motunrayo Odusanya

Program & Activities

Dolly Children Foundation has the following major programs:

- Dolly Stars School: A Tuition-free school for marginalised children

- Edufuture Conference: The vision for this conference is rooted in the belief that Africa's immense potential can be realised through education. The event serves as a platform for diaogue, collaboration within the development sector.

- Weekly reading clubs in primary schools. This weekly event has benefited over 10000 children till date.

- Sponsor a Child Initiative: Dolly Children Foundation has provided sponsorship in educational aid and welfare to over 10,200 at-risk children by paying tuition fees, providing school kits such as uniforms, bags, and shoes and delivering learning materials.

- Teacher training. We have conducted series of workshops and training for public school teachers so as to expose them to the 21st century teaching experiences. Over 2500 teachers from publc and low income schools have ben trained in DCF workshops.

About The Author

Adedolapo Osuntuyi is the founder of Dolly Children Foundation; a nonprofit organisation which focuses on inspiring the African Child to adopt 21st century skills through education, capacity building and advocacy programmes. Her deep passion for empowering children from low–income backgrounds to achieve equal opportunities was borne out of the personal experiences of her dad in his early years. Her work in the foundation where she leads the organizational strategy and management has impacted over 22,000 children in 25 communities in 4 states.

Dolapo has over 14 years' experience in child protection, early childhood and community development programs. She is a graduate of Botany from the Lagos State University and holds a Master's Degree in Child Health & Social Care from the prestigious University of Central Lancashire, Preston, United Kingdom. In 2015, she received an Africa – America Institute Scholarship to study Social Sector Management Course at the Enterprise Development Centre, Pan – Atlantic University, Nigeria.

In 2021, Dolapo was recognized as one of the 50 African Women in Development. She has been featured on a number of platforms, news periodicals and has received several awards and nominations including a community service award from the Enugu State Government. In 2017, she became a fellow of the Young African Leaders Initiative, West Africa Regional Centre, a US Government Initiative and one of the best three awardees of her cohort in the Women in Management, Business and Public service (WIMBIZ) Mentorship program. She works with public and private schools to facilitates educational based programmes with core competencies in policymaking, child behavioural development and educational management.

Dolapo also serves as a director on the board of UPIG Development Foundation and is the Mums Coordinator for Social Good Lagos (an initiative of the United Nations Foundation). She is also a volunteer Mentor with Teach for Nigeria.

Dolapo believes that every child is a star and has chosen to play her part in ensuring that no child is left behind because of race, class and ethnicity.

The Hands That Help and Lift

Hearts and Hands

Printed in Great Britain
by Amazon